Green Gardening

Ideas To Potter Around With

BENITA SEN

Illustrated by **VANDANA BIST**

HarperCollins*Children'sBooks*

HarperCollins PUBLISHERS

First published in India in 2017 by HarperCollins Children's Books
An imprint of HarperCollins *Publishers*
Building No 10, Tower A, 4th Floor, DLF Cyber City, Phase II,
Gurugram – 122002
www.harpercollins.co.in

2 3 4 5 6 7 8 9 10

P-ISBN: 978-93-5277-430-2

Typeset in Comfortaa font by Mukesh Kumar Aggarwal

Printed and bound at Nutech Print Services - India

Contents

Get Going, Get Growing, Get Making

Gardening and crafts can get you humming. They are both happy-happy hobbies and healthy-happy hobbies. But do be careful when you are gardening or when you are making something for your garden.

- Work when an adult is around so that if you need help, it will be at hand.
- Avoid sharp instruments. For instance, instead of pointed scissors, use a pair with rounded edges.
- Wear gloves for safety. Wash your hands thoroughly with soap even if you use gloves. If you garden without gloves, make sure to scrub under your nails after you are done.
- Work neat. Whether you are gardening or crafting, your workspace should not be littered. Working in an untidy place could cause mistakes and injury.
- Never rest anything sharp on the ground or on a chair. This can injure someone. Keep sharp instruments in a case or on a table.
- Which is more fun: growing plants from seeds or making things for your garden? Find out for yourself! But when you buy a packet of seeds, go to a well-known shop since it will probably have healthier seeds. Check the date on the packet to make sure the seeds are fresh, because old seeds may not sprout.
- Check out a hobby store for a children's gardening kit. Try to use implements that are lighter and less sharp.

Green Gardening

Ways to reduce waste and re-use more as you work those green fingers

Note For Parents And Teachers

Children and young adults need supervision while gardening and/or crafting. Some plants or parts of plants can be poisonous and even fatal. If you are not sure, ask a specialist or steer clear of an unknown plant. Even common, easy-growing plants such as dieffenbachia (dumb cane) are best kept away from children and pets. Growing plants in logs of wood may encourage mushrooms to sprout. These may be poisonous.

- Castor
- Croton
- Common oleander
- Yellow oleander
- Datura
- Cassava
- Dieffenbachia

Disclaimer

Watch out: Gardening and making things are fun, but you could injure yourself when you handle implements. So always have a responsible adult around when you potter about among plants or get crafting.

For parents and teachers: Adult supervision is advised while gardening and/or making the crafts given in this book to avoid any untoward incident.

If you're in a dry, dusty, dreary desert, what's the most cheerful, soothing colour you look for? **Green!** Sadly, most of our towns and cities are growing so fast, they have left very little space for trees and plants, parks and gardens. If we're not careful, we may soon be living in urban deserts. Each of us can add a touch of green in our own lives and decorate our little garden with things around us.

Did you ask, *why*?

As more and more of us pack ourselves into towns and cities, our homes and gardens are getting smaller. In fact, many of us are perched metres above the ground, in high-rise apartments. Does that mean we give up on gardening? Not quite. We can garden almost anywhere. Look again at a balcony, window box or even a windowsill. There's always space for a few plants in every home.

So, while plants would be happiest being planted in the ground, in most gardens today, we use flower pots or containers.

Humans have always lived near plants. Even if we don't want to eat the plants we grow, having plants around keeps us healthy and happy. Plants give us oxygen, which we breathe in to stay alive. Even though plants take in water to make their food and to stay alive, they release most of that water back into the air as water vapour, which helps keep the air around them moist. Moist air keeps our skin from drying.

Off With That Cough!

If you have plants around you, chances are, you cough less than does a friend in a home without plants!

The air around us is full of poisons or toxins. They are found in most things we use, from plastic bags to ink, paint and synthetic carpets. Plants can clear the air of these toxins. This makes plants our friends.

Just having plants around at home or in school can keep people more cheerful and healthy.

NASA Knows!

In 1989, NASA (National Aeronautics and Space Administration, USA), the organization that sends shuttles into space, studied house plants and found that plants rid the air of harmful chemicals such as benzene, formaldehyde and trichloroethylene.

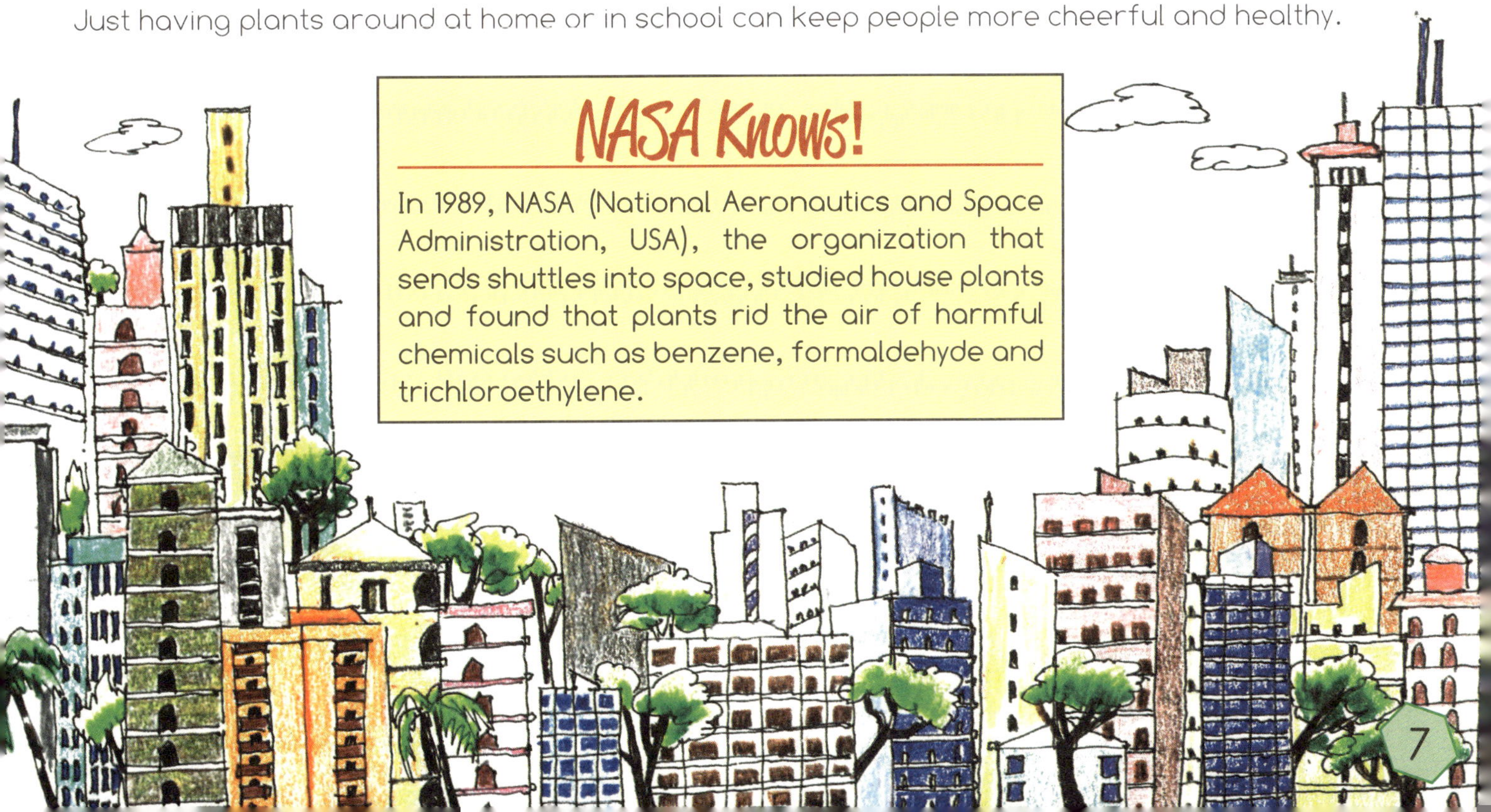

Grow Smart

- Agave plants (*Agave*)
- Aloe (*Aloe vera*)[1]
- Chinese evergreen (*Aglaonema*)
- Dracaena: warneckei, marginata, Janet Craig (*Darcaena*)
- English ivy (*Hedera helix*)
- Flapjacks (*Kalanchoe thyrsiflora*)
- *Haworthia*
- Hens and chicks (*Echeveria elegans*)[2]
- Jade plant (*Crassula ovate*)[3]
- *Kalanchoe*
- Money plant (*Pothos*)
- Peace Lily (*Spathiphyllum*)
- *Philodendron*
- Purple heart (*Tradescantia pallid*)
- Radiator plant (*Peperomia*)
- Rubber plant (*Ficus elastica*)
- Schefflera (*Schefflera arboricola*)
- Snake plant/Mother-in-law's tongue (*Sansevieria trifasciata*)
- Spider plant (*Chlorophytum comosum*)
- Zee Zee (*Zamioculcas zamiifolia*)

- Vinca
- Ipomoea
- Kochia
- Zinnia

- Marigold
- Chrysanthemum

- Petunia
- Nasturtium
- Salvia
- Calendula

1. http://www.med-health.net/Aloe-Vera.html
2. http://www.lovethatimage.com/blog/2013/05/turquoise-succulent/
3. http://lawnpatiobarn.wordpress.com/tag/jade-plant/

Vegetables

- Ladies finger (bhindi)
- Brinjal (baigan)
- Gourd (tori, lauki)
- Pumpkin (kaddu)

- Spinach (palak)
- Fenugreek (methi)
- Beans
- Flat beans (seem)
- Tomato
- Mustard (sarson)
- Lettuce

WHERE IS THE MUD?

Gone are the days when you planted only in mud. Now, potting soil is becoming popular among garden enthusiasts. One reason is that mud is hard to find for city-slickers. Another reason is that potting soil is mixed and treated to keep plants healthy and free from disease. Some potting mixes have fertilizer and nutrients mixed in them.

However, if you still want to use good old soil, try to balance the texture and nutrients. Most plants do well with:

Cacti and succulents will need more sand and some gravel, and less soil.

Craft 1
Potter Around With Pots

What's the most important thing needed to start gardening? A plant, of course.

Next comes soil.

After that on the list, for a growing number of gardeners, is a flower pot. Those who don't live on the ground floor need a container to put the plant in.

Terracotta or earthen pots are the most common. Terracotta is made by mixing mud with water. The mixture is then turned on a potter's wheel to make the pot. After the pot has dried in the sun, it is baked in an oven called a kiln. This makes it hard.

But it can still break. So, what do we do with a broken flower pot? Throw it into the garbage?

No! There are fun things you could do with the pot! Take a good look at it. Do you see what we saw – a new pot? You can re-use a broken pot to be a little kinder to the local landfill where trash gets dumped.

Any tub that houses a plant needs a drainage hole at the bottom or on the side to let extra water out. With a broken pot, you don't need to worry about that!

What You Need

- A broken terracotta pot
- Soil
- Pebbles and broken bits of terracotta or tile
- Broken-brick colour (geru) or leftover waterproof paint
- Brush

What You Need To Do

- Paint the pot. Block the drainage hole at the bottom of the pot with the broken bits from the pot. This will prevent the mud and the nutrients from being washed out when you water the plant. Since this plug is made of terracotta, it will still let the extra water seep out so that the roots don't drown.
- Tilt the pot back and fill half of it with soil.
- Place the plant inside and cover the roots with more soil.
- Wondering what to do with the broken front? Push pebbles or more broken terracotta pieces in to make a holding wall.
- Tilt the pot back a little, balancing it with pebbles, so that only a little water flows out.

Top Tip

More than one broken pot? Place the pots one over the other using an old aluminium rod to make a tall arrangement.

What You Could Plant

Since some water will leach out, a plant that does not need much water, such as a cactus, would be perfect.

I LOVE TERRACOTTA

Why planting in terracotta is awesome:

- It is porous. The tiny holes let air in, keep the plant cooler than a plastic or cement pot would, and let extra water out. This can save the plant, since many of us pour in too much water, drowning the roots and making the plant ill.
- Terracotta doesn't heat up or cool down too fast, so the roots don't frazzle in summers, nor do they freeze in winters.
- Since every part of the pot is porous, every part of the plant below the surface can breathe easy.
- If you live in a high-rise apartment, lighter plastic pots may be knocked down by the wind, but the heavier terracotta ones will stay put. Secure all pots anyway.
- In most places, terracotta is made by hand so when you buy terracotta, you support a craftsperson and you support a craft that is thousands of years old!

Craft 2
That's My Planter

As cities grow, it is getting difficult and expensive to get planters. But you can make gardening more fun and spend less money on pots! Almost any vessel or container that is no longer wanted in the house can be turned into an unusual planter.

What You Need

- **Empty plastic bottle**
- **Pen**
- **Soil (mix equal parts of earth, sand and leaf mould, or buy potting mix)**
- **Plants (plants of one kind look better in one bottle)**
- **Pair of scissors**

What You Need To Do

- Wash and clean the plastic bottle. With a pen, mark 8 to 12 spots in a pattern around and under the bottle. Cut holes around each mark. You may need to ask an adult to help with this.

- Push the roots of the plants carefully through the holes, one spot for one plant. Open the bottle cap and fill the bottle with soil. Make sure the soil is filled tight by pushing it down with your finger or with the pen. Tap the bottle once in a while to help the soil settle. Water your unusual planter with a little water at a time. As the soil settles, top up with more.

- **TIP:** If you find too much water flowing out, push pebbles into the holes. This will allow excess water to flow out, but help most of the soil to stay in.

What You Could Plant

Perennials or long-lasting plants such as hens and chicks or money plant; summer seasonals such as portulaca; or winter seasonals such as pansy and nasturtium.

Craft 3
Medley Magic

What You Need

- Crate (used to cart fizzy drinks)
- Old plastic bags
- Soil or potting mix
- Pebbles
- Broken tiles
- Small plants like hens and chicks, wandering Jew, mother-in-law's tongue, hajar dana
- Leftover lengths of clothesline cord

What You Need To Do

- Clean out the crate.
- Plan the arrangement. Filling every compartment would make the arrangement too cluttered. Instead, look at the four corners and the centre. At most, you could include a few more in between. Place the plants on the spots you want to plant them. Don't like what you see? Move the plants around till you see a pattern you like.
- Cut the plastic bag large enough to line one compartment. Before you place it, make a snip or two at the bottom for excess water to drain out. Fill the lined compartments with soil.
- To plant, push down the soil at the centre of each chosen compartment. Place the roots of the plant in it. Cover with soil and gently push down so that the potting mix holds the plant tight. When all the plants have been housed, line the top of the vacant sections with pebbles.
- Block the open sides with broken tiles. Tie the two lengths of cord to the side handles and hang the unusual planter. Remember, the pebbles and plants may fall out if the crate hangs at 90 degrees, so tilt it back a little.

Craft 4
Nuts And Dots

Drink Up!

Coconut water is healthier than any artificial drink. It is low in calories. There is more potassium in one coconut than there is in a couple of bananas, so it is good for our heart, nerves, muscles and kidneys. It helps us digest food. It is better than any sports drink.

Most of us love drinking coconut water. But have you ever observed a coconut seller's stall? Often, there are empty coconut shells lying around. If the vendor is careful, there will be a dustbin at hand. Sadly, most stalls don't have one, so the empty shells roll around, littering the street. But we can help the environment by using these coconut shells in our garden!

What You Need

- Empty coconut shell
- Soil and sand
- Dry leaves or leaf mould
- Plant
- Paint (leftover wood paint will do)
- Brush
- Wire or sturdy cord (three pieces – two 28-inch pieces and one about 14 inches, enough to go around the coconut)
- Vermicompost (optional)

What You Need To Do

- Clean the empty coconut shell with tap water. Don't worry if there is some white flesh lining the insides. It will decompose and become a source of nutrition for the plant.
- Paint the outside of the shell. Let it dry. This should take a day or two, depending on the weather and on where you set it to dry. If you don't paint the shell, your natural planting pot will shrivel up and become unusable faster.
- On a piece of newspaper, place a handful of soil, one clutch of dry leaves, two fistfuls of sand and one part vermicompost (optional), which you can buy from a nursery. If you don't want to make the mixture yourself, you can simply buy potting mix from a nursery.
- Fill the coconut with this potting mix, till about the width of one finger from the top. This space will allow water to seep in gently when you water the plant.
- Since water cannot drain out of the sides or the bottom of this container, mixing sand and leaf mould will make sure the soil doesn't get too soggy. Too much water could rot the roots.
- Dent the soil with a finger and place the roots of the plant in it. Cover the roots with soil. Pat down so that the soil is firm. Pour a little water.
- Tightly wrap the shorter wire/cord around the coconut, a couple of inches from the top. Now, loop one end of the 28-inch wire around one side of the girdle you just tied, and the other end around the girdle on the opposite side. Repeat with the third piece of wire about 90 degrees away from the first two ties. This will give you two long wire grips.
- Hang the coconut planter from a balcony or a window, preferably in a spot that gets a few hours of sun.

What You Could Plant

Unlike a broken pot, the coconut shell won't allow any water to drain out. So, go for plants that don't mind soaking their feet a little, such as the money plant. Before watering, stick a finger into the soil to check if it is dry. If the soil feels moist, you can postpone watering.

Craft 5
Stakes Are High

Some plants need a little help to stand straight and tall. A stick in the soil near the plant can be the right support. But sticks can look rather boring, so let's get creative!

What Nou Need

- **About 36 inches of any leftover aluminium pipe or lengths of grass reed, such as sircanda**
- **Leftover wool, ribbon or tape**
- **Adhesive**
- **Pair of scissors**
- **Leftover baubles**

What You Need To Do

- Clean the pipe.
- Lay out the wool or ribbon in a colour scheme of your choice.
- Beginning at one end, slather about 3 inches of the surface of the pipe with adhesive. Lay the end of the first ribbon along these 3 inches, going all the way to the end.
- Beginning at this end, wrap the ribbon tightly around the pipe, patting it into place to make sure the adhesive sticks.
- As you come to the end of the 3 inches of adhesive, smear the next 3 inches or so with adhesive and keep wrapping the ribbon.

- When you come to the end of the first length of ribbon, lay the last inch or so vertically along the pipe.
- Repeat with the second length of tape or wool or ribbon, winding it carefully over the vertical inch of the first ribbon when you begin.
- The more colours you use, the brighter will be the stick. But remember not to cover the last 6 inches of the pipe since it will be under the soil.
- Decorate the top end with baubles.
- Push the bare end of the stick into the soil near a plant that needs support.
- Be careful not to damage the roots. Let the plant rest against the stick, or tie it to the stick with a loose bow to hold it in place.

A truly green gardener will not harm a live plant for decoration. If you can't find a metal stick, go scouring for dry twigs that have fallen off a tree.

Craft 6
Bottled Joy

What's a garden without some decorations? Rescue things that are about to end up in the trash can and re-use them to jazz up your garden.

What You Need

- Six old bottles in different sizes
- Six stakes, such as old knitting needles, aluminium pipes, iron rods
- Leftover paint, from painting doors and windows
- Thick, flat paint brush
- Wads made from 6 inch x 6 inch newspapers folded twice
- Flower pot filled with soil
- Tape

What You Need To Do

- Paint each bottle. It will be easy to paint if you hold up the bottle on a finger. Set the bottle out to dry by placing it on its neck.
- Paint each stake. Leave the last 6 inches since this will be under the soil. To dry the paint, insert each stake into the soil at an angle, up to the point where the painted part starts.
- Tape a wad of paper over the end of the stake to protect the bottle when you crown it. Carefully cap each stake with an inverted bottle.

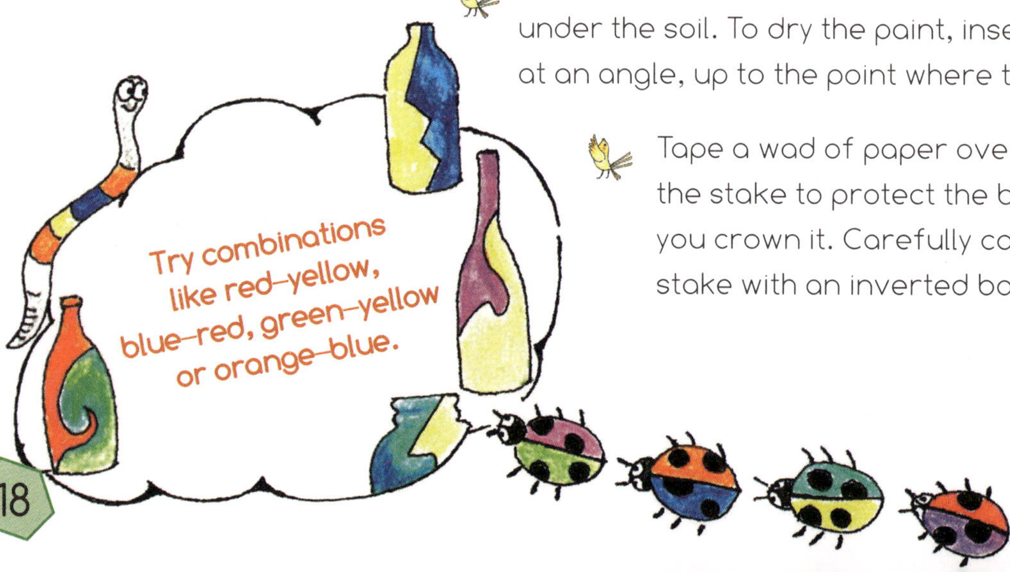

Craft 7
Roomy Old Shoe

What You Need

- Roomy old shoes, such as Crocs or boots
- Potting mix or soil
- Plant

What You Need To Do

- Fill the shoe with potting mix till a couple of inches from the top.
- Shape a hole in the middle of the soil and place the roots of the plant in it. Fill the dent with soil and pat the soil to remove any air pockets that could dry out the roots.
- Lightly water the soil around the plant.

What You Could Plant

Crocs do not retain too much water, so use a succulent such as kalanchoe.

If you are planting in an old boot, try ferns that may tolerate more water. Remember, most ferns don't like direct sunlight.

Craft 8
Birds – Take a Bow

What's a garden without birds? Quiet, boring – that's what! And missing all the help that birds bring to plants.

Birds and plants have lived together for millions of years. But now, as our cities and towns grow larger and our fields are full of harmful chemical pesticides and fertilizers, their habitat is shrinking. So, we owe it to birds to provide them with safe food, water and shelter.

Birds are handy around the garden. Insect-eating birds such as bulbuls keep gardens pest-free, so we can avoid dangerous chemicals. Birds that feed on nectar help pollinate flowers. Birds such as sparrows often pick out weeds or plants we don't want around. That saves us from the work of weeding the flower beds! The twitter and songs of birds help us relax.

THE EASIEST BIRD FEEDER

Birds get their food from planted areas. Seed eaters, such as sparrows, have lived around our homes for ages, feeding off grain that we drop while sifting, packing and moving the grain. As old-world sacks are replaced with spill-proof plastic-lined bags, it is difficult for these birds to find food.

So, let's invite them home to a feast!

What You Need

- An unused, small basket about 8 inches across
- Two strips of ribbon, each about 6 feet long
- One strip of ribbon about 6 inches long
- Grain (bird seed, bajra, broken wheat or broken rice)

What You Need To Do

- Clean out the basket with a cloth duster.
- Pick a point (A) on the edge of the basket and tie one end of the first ribbon to it. Tie the other end to the point opposite point A.
- Turn the basket 90 degrees and repeat with the second ribbon.
- Hold the centre of both the ribbon loops together, and tie them with the shorter ribbon.
- Fill half the basket with grain and hang it from a height.
- Carefully decide where you want to put up the feeder. Make sure your feathered friends are safe from cats and dogs.
- If the bottom is woven loosely, grain will fall out. You can line the basket with paper or plastic before adding the grain.
- Top up the grain in the feeder regularly. Make sure the grain is clean, fresh and dry.
- Wet grain can become infected with fungus and make the bird very sick.

Craft 9
The Second-Easiest Bird Feeder

What You Need

- An empty juice carton
- Pair of scissors and a cutter
- Stick
- Adhesive
- Pencil
- Wool needle
- Twine

What You Need To Do

- Wash the carton thoroughly. Set it out to dry. Do not paint the carton. While a painted carton looks nice, paints often contain chemicals that can harm the birds if they eat some by mistake. Some paints even emit harmful chemicals.
- Pull up the top of the carton into the shape of a sloping roof.
- Halfway down the front of the carton, cut out a door-like opening. If this seems dfficult, take an adult's help. Make a hole with the scissors just below the door and push the stick in to make a perch.
- Ask an adult to help you thread the needle with twine and push it through the top of the carton. Tie the ends in a knot to make a loop for hanging the feeder.
- Your bird feeder is now ready to house grain and welcome birds.

Craft 10
Fish-Bowl Garden

More and more people want to set caged birds free or take a goldfish out of a bowl and place it in a larger tank. But before you throw the empty cage or the fish bowl into the garbage, take a second look. You could turn the fish bowl into a terrarium or a mini-garden. A terrarium is often sown in a glass bowl that can be covered with a glass lid. When the plants grow too big for the space, you can shift them to a larger pot and put small plants in their place.

What You Need

- Fish bowl
- A handful of charcoal pieces
- Potting mix
- Small plants, preferably succulents that grow slowly
- Moss

What You Need To Do

- A fish bowl is an unusual planter. There is no hole in it for extra water to drain out of. So, line the bottom with about 2 inches of charcoal pieces. They will absorb water.

- Fill half the bowl with potting soil. Make little dents in the soil, and in each dent, place a plant. Cover the roots with soil and pat firmly. Spread moss over the soil. The moss will keep the soil moist longer. Sprinkle a little water from the top. Some terrariums or glass-bowl gardens are covered and need less water. If you plan not to cover the glass-bowl garden, water it whenever the soil feels dry. Don't forget to place your unusual garden somewhere it will get at least three to four hours of indirect sunlight. Glass heats up much faster than a terracotta tub, so a glass terrarium garden is ideal for a room. Since a terrarium is a closed garden, watch the plants carefully. Remove dry leaves and flowers. If a plant looks ill, move it out into a regular pot before it dies or infects the others.

What You Could Plant

Slow-growing plants such as succulents. Try sedum, kalanchoe or echeveria.

Craft 11
Set the Greenery Free

What You Need

- Old bird cage
- Plastic sheet
- Felt pen
- Pair of scissors
- Soil
- Coconut fibre
- Plants
- Hook

Don't have an old cage? Ask your local store for an old egg basket!

What You Need To Do

- Clean the bird cage. Place the cage at the centre of the plastic sheet and outline its shape.
- Remove the cage and draw another line about 5 inches above the first line.
- Cut the plastic around the outer line. Make a few tiny holes around the centre of the sheet. Excess water will drain out from here.
- Line the bottom and a few inches of the side with the plastic sheet.
- Place a layer of coconut husk over the sheet and top it with potting mix or soil.
- Make dents in the soil and place the plant roots in the dents. Pat the soil firmly around the roots. Water the plants. Hang the cage where the plants will get enough light to grow and glow.

What You Could Plant

Slow-growing plants such as succulents. Try sedum, kalanchoe or echeveria, or trailing plants such as money plant.

Craft 12
Now, Make a Splash!

Every living thing needs water. Birds and insects are no exceptions. They need a steady source of clean water through the year, even in winter. It is not enough to put up a bird bath or water bowl. You must make sure that it is kept in a place where the bird is safe from enemies, such as cats and dogs, and where it has a little privacy, like the corner of a window garden, behind plants. Keep the bowl in a fixed place so that the birds don't have to look for it every day. Change the water at least once a day or whenever you see that it is dirty to ensure that the birds always have clean water to drink.

What You Need

- **Three to four terracotta flower pots**
- **Earthen plate with a 3-inch high rim**
- **Water**
- **Sticks**

Decorate the outside of the pots with leftover paint, or stick on old clips, buttons, baubles and pebbles.

What You Need To Do

- Clean the flower pots with water or cloth. When they are dry, set them upside down. Make a tower of pots with the largest pot at the bottom. Place the plate on top of the last pot.
- Fill the plate with water. Float a couple of sticks in the water for insects to perch on.

Craft 13
Mini Magic

Short of space? Not sure what to do with your baby bath tub? Don't throw it away! Keep the memories in your own mini-garden.

What You Need

- Old, large tub
- Potting mix or soil
- Small plants
- 6 inch x 6 inch grass patch (bought from a nursery or cut out from a field)
- Pebbles, marbles, broken bangles, broken pots, old toys, old toy furniture, old tealight holders
- Pair of scissors

What You Need To Do

- Does the tub have a crack or a hole? Use that as the draining hole to let out extra water. To prevent too much water from flowing out, line the opening with pieces of broken pots.
- If the tub has no existing cracks or holes, ask an adult to help you make a few at the bottom. These will then work as water outlets. Cover them with pebbles and terracotta pieces so the soil does not block them.

Fill the tub with potting mix or soil suitable for the plants you have in mind. Stop a couple of inches short of the rim to leave a little space for water. Try to choose plants that are from the same family, such as evergreens or succulents, so that the soil and water requirements are almost the same. Before creating the mini-garden, try out various arrangements of plants and decorations till you are sure you like the picture.

Place a patch of grass to make your own little lawn. Then, in the soil surrounding the patch, make a little hole with your finger and place the roots of a plant in it. Close the hole with more soil and pat firmly. Repeat till all the plants are in place. Add decorations. If you don't have miniature furniture, you could make your own: fashion a fence by tying ice-cream sticks loosely with string; place two broken bangles an inch apart to make a little bridge.

Planting Tips

- Plants are living things. Most gardeners have killed a few plants by mistake or because they didn't know enough, but they try their best to keep the plants healthy. To ensure that your plants are healthy, read up or ask keen gardeners how to best care for them. Some of the most knowledgeable people could be the people you buy the plant from.

- When you buy a plant, note its name, the amount of sunlight it needs and how frequently to water it.

- For most of the seasons in India, the best time of day to plant is in the evening around dusk so that the plant can get its breath back before the next day's harsh sunlight.

- Prepare the soil before you plant. Plants take their food from the soil, so try to find out what kind of soil your plant prefers. If you plant a cactus in soil meant for a water reed, it will fall sick.

- Planting a sapling? Dig out enough earth to house the roots and part of the stem. Wet the hole with a little water. Ease the roots into their new home. Cover with soil. Pat the soil down firmly so that there are no air pockets that can dry out the roots. Water the plant lightly.

- Many of us kill plants with our love and too much water. Before you water the plant, check the soil with your finger. If the top 2 inches feel dry, it is time to water.

WH-EE(D) With Plants

FEED is what plants do for us, don't they? We need to feed plants nutrients too. Ask a nurseryman what and when to feed a particular plant.

GREED is what pushes us to ask for more while the Earth gets less.

HEED is what we need to do when experts tell us to grow more plants and to save green lives.

LEED or **Leadership in Energy and Environmental Design** is a programme that teaches us to think of less harmful ways to build houses.

MEED is a reward. That's what plants are for humans!

NEED, as in we need plants around us if we are to stay alive.

REED is a kind of plant that is really a tall grass.

SEED is what plants grow from.

WEED is a plant for which we have not found a use, so we believe it useless.

Colour Your Garden

Colour Your Garden

Benita Sen is a journalist and children's author, who has authored a popular gardening column in a newspaper. A trained educationist, she conducts workshops for young people on environmental issues. Her various passions and experience in the outdoors come together in this book of simple, workable ideas she has tried and tested – ideas that can turn even a windowsill into a garden.

Vandana Bist has been working as an illustrator since 1985, for varied genres of writing, with special emphasis on children's books, particularly picture books and textbooks. In 2014, she began a venture called **AkkaBakka**, to combine art, writing, storytelling, music and theatre and to create workshop modules for children of various age groups. Vandana lives in Delhi.